Behind The Smile
a journey to strength

Stephanie Betts

This book is dedicated to all the people who struggle with the scars of an abusive past. Although you cannot undo the past, you can live for the future. Make the commitment to become *Freedom Focused.*

I want the smile that you display so easily to be real. Allow my Word to turn your smile real. Happiness comes from me. As you walk in joy and happiness through my Word, you will begin to experience my fullness that you have been longing for.

God (2010)

Bible Translations used...
King James Version (KJV)
New Living Translation (NLT)
New King James Version (NKJV)
New International Version (NIV)

Table of Content

Prelude...

A smile can be defined as a warm and inviting facial expression that alludes to a personal state of happiness, good fortune, or pleasure. A smile can often break the ice in tense situations; and can even serve as a silent "welcome", inviting someone into your domain or space.

Still, in some cases, and more specifically, in my case, a smile was nothing more than a veil covering fear, hurt, disappointment and pain; a clever disguise, worn to ward off any questions.

This is my story...

And they overcame him by the blood of the Lamb and by the word of their testimony; and they loved not their lives unto the death.
Revelations 12:11 (KJV)

Introduction...

In a perfect world, all parents would love their children the way God loves his, unconditionally and without change. In this same world, all children would be viewed as gifts from heaven, little miracles that will one day grow into world changers. In a perfect world, all parents would count it an honor to be chosen to raise and rear a child, entrusted with a precious opportunity to train up the most valuable asset the human race has to offer to themselves and to God, future generations.

Unfortunately, in our not-so-perfect world, most children are considered mistakes or obstacles that cost too much, take up too much time, and consume far too much attention and energy. In our not-so-perfect world, these kids end up abused, forgotten, neglected, or in state custody. I know this all too well, because I myself was one of these burdens.

Most cases of child abuse and neglect go unreported, and over 80 percent of child abusers are parents or a relative. Neglect is the most common form of child abuse; followed by physical abuse, sexual abuse, psychological abuse, and lastly, medical neglect. Many families look past what could be considered some of the most obvious characteristics of a neglected and abused child; chronic fatigue, weight loss or weight gain, chronic pain, anxiety, withdrawal, sadness and quietness.

Behind the Smile shares my experiences with neglect, as well as physical, sexual and psychological abuse during my childhood. This is the story of how I coped, and eventually had the courage to demand the abuse stop. This book is not about blame, but about embracing a process, and in time, healing from the scars of abuse, low self-esteem, and lack of trust… And yes, there is a happy ending; one founded on the realization that Jesus Christ had been with me all along, even when I was in too much pain to acknowledge His presence. The hell I experienced couldn't negate God's ultimate plans for my good. This is a tell all story of how the love of the Savior allowed me to heal and taught me to forgive.

Chapter 1... The Beginning

> *Before I formed thee in the belly I knew thee; and*
> *before thou camest forth out of the womb I sanctified thee, and*
> *I ordained thee a prophet unto the nations.*
>
> *Jeremiah 1:15 (KJV)*

In order to appreciate my ending, we'll have to start from the beginning. You see, while some little girls are busy playing princess and planning tea parties, I knew better than to make the kind of noise these games required. Instead of lightheartedly experimenting in my mom's make-up or stampeding through our home in high heel shoes that were 5 sizes too large, I was being careful to tread lightly, well versed in the do's and don'ts of living with an alcoholic mother.

The house was often dark, and mom was usually in her room with the door closed. As I looked from my bedroom window, I noticed the sun going down and wondered if I would get to eat soon. I'd often press my ear against that closed bedroom door and hear her snoring.

"Will she wake up?" I thought to myself. "My stomach hurts." Gently, I'd tap on the door, but no movement. Not too loud, or I might wake her and then she'd be angry. I didn't want my mother to be angry. I knew that being quiet was a must at all times. "Oh God, please let her wake up so that I can eat." I cried out in my head. No stranger to severe hunger pains, I knew what needed to be done. I made my way to the bathroom, and putting my head under the faucet I drank and drank until my stomach felt full. Once I was sure I'd drank enough water to calm my raging belly, I lay down in my bed and fell asleep feeling so alone.

It's been said, that feelings of loneliness can often be considered normal or to be expected for an only child; but in my case, being an only child with a single parent, alcoholic mother felt like total isolation. I often found myself wishing I had a brother or sister. I thought that if I at least had a sibling, then I wouldn't have to experience such a horrible existence by myself. I'd even sometimes cry in anguish, hoping my absent father would somehow hear me from wherever he was and come rescue me from my mother.

Why did she hate me so? I was a good girl... I was quiet and careful to never ask for anything. Still, she said she hated me. I learned much later in life that she hated me because my father left her. He didn't help her support me financially, and she felt robbed of her youth. Had she not have gotten pregnant, her life would never have ended in the mess she felt it was in. I was her burden rather than a blessing. When she looked at me, the only thing she seemed to feel was regret. I was a constant reminder of the mistake she made with my father...

Chapter 2... Love That Hurts

But even the very hairs of your head are all numbered. Fear not therefore: ye are of more value than many sparrows.

St. Luke 12:7 (KJV)

There is uniqueness about the capacity of children to love. They seem to faithfully continue loving, even when mistreated or abused. Unfortunately, this makes them easy and ideal prey. Perhaps it's their innocence that predators seek out, and this same innocence that makes predators believe their wrongs will go undiscovered.

Still, if you look closely enough, abused and neglected children have a distinct look about them. These subtle life and death signs and silent cries of distress are often overlooked or simply brushed under a rug. There's a look that children give you, sadness in their eyes, when they know an adult is doing something wrong to them, but they're too afraid to tell someone. There's a look that cries out for help that abused children often carry well into adulthood. I know that look well, because I carried it most of my life...

Unfortunately, instead of making me stick out like a sore thumb, the look seemed to make me that much more invisible. I look back now and wonder whether or not my teachers, my grandparents, or the neighbors suspected anything… There are memories that stick out in my mind each time I've asked myself the question.

This particular day as my mother dropped me off at the front door of my school, I remember carrying that same heaviness and sadness I'd grown accustomed too. I don't remember much about the school other than not liking my teacher. Like my mother, she seemed to have a knack for overlooking me, so school wasn't much of an escape from my already lonely existence.

While my teachers and the appearance of my school building didn't leave enough of an impression to remember, I do remember the school age years of my life being horrible. I was so on edge that I suffered from chronic stomach pains. My mother took me to several doctors to no avail. I know now that those pains were from my constant worrying. Would this be a normal day? Would she be in a good mood?

This day I said goodbye as my mother pulled away, and began to suck my thumb on my way to the school doors. Though my mother despised it, I'd sucked my thumb for as long as I could remember. I didn't care how odd it looked at my age; it was the one comfort no one could take away from me. Of course, that didn't stop my mother from trying everything from hot sauce to tape on my thumbs to stop me.

Appearing out of what seemed to be thin air, I heard my mother yelling from behind me. I'd just known the coast was clear for one last rendezvous with my thumb, and distinctly remembered watching her drive away! "Get in the car!" she yelled. Both startled and surprised, I responded in fearful obedience and quickly got back into the car.

My mother began to hit me repeatedly with her fist yelling, "YOU ARE NOT A BABY!" The whole thing happened so fast, I think I was more stunned than hurt! Still beating me, she told me to pull myself together and get out of the car. Although I'd begun crying hysterically, I somehow managed to do exactly what I was told and walked quietly into the school doors. This was one of many spontaneous outbursts that had become all too familiar.

In spite of how dreadful my existence seemed to be, I only worked up the nerve to run away once. I remember it like yesterday. The day was nothing special, typical even. After one of my mother's usual drinking sprees she had fallen asleep in the middle of the afternoon. However, this particular day my mother had agreed to pick my cousin up from school and was sleeping right through her obligation... I of course knew we needed to pick my cousin up, but was terrified at the thought of waking my mother. It might as well have been an unspoken rule in our house that you DO NOT wake my mother for any reason, and come hell or high water, I wasn't risking another beating, even for my cousin's sake.

I paced the floor, frantically pondering what I should do. The phone began to ring and my mother woke up yelling for me to come downstairs. In a panic, she yelled, "Let's go!", and we took of down the street in our car. Yelling the whole car ride, she scolded me for not waking her when I knew she had to pick my cousin up from school. She warned me that she was going to beat me as soon as we returned home. "Not another beating", I thought, as my stomach begin to twist and turn into knots.

We soon arrived at my cousin's school and were driving back to our house. As we turned the corner on our street I could not stop shaking. Not another beating! In a split second my fight or flight reflex kicked in and everything changed. In what seemed like a Hollywood production or some sort of out of body experience, I found myself bolting out of the car as we pulled into the driveway. I ran down the street! Running! Running! Running! I ran until my block was a distant scene in the rearview mirror of my mind.

Now what? I didn't have any place to go, and I didn't know my way around... "What have I done?!" I thought. How would I eat? So many thoughts and fears began to flood my mind; and I had no answers. Somehow the fear of attempting to survive alone with no place to go, begin to grow more looming than the thought of being beaten. I'm not quite sure how long I stayed away, but I eventually found myself walking back down the block toward the only home I'd known. Some kid ran up to me and asked my name. I told her, and she grabbed my arm and yelled, "Here she is!", as she dragged me the rest of the way to my house.

Neighbors standing in their front yards lined the block glaring at me and shaking their heads. I was surprised any of them knew what I had done. I found it funny that so many of them had no idea what I was enduring at home, and no concern for what I'd run away from to begin with; yet they all looked at me like such a bad girl.

Just then, in another scene straight from a Hollywood production, my mother hugged me as though she was so relieved I was home and took me into the house. She handed me the telephone with my grandparents on the other end asking if I was okay and wanting to know why I'd run away. I told them I didn't know… I would have told them anything but the truth. I knew they lived too far away, and if I told, they wouldn't be able to get there fast enough to protect me from the beating I was sure would follow that confession.

My mother sat me down on the couch and told me never to run away again. It was as though in spite of her hatred toward me, I belonged at home with her. She asked if I was hungry, and when I responded yes, she answered, "Too bad", and sent me to bed.

Over the next week or two, as punishment my meals consisted of boiled rice with black pepper and a glass of water. Every meal was the same, boiled rice, black pepper, and water. My mother forced me to sit at the table until I'd finished it all. I'd rather have gone hungry than to keep eating that rice. I once attempted to

hide the rice in the garbage, but my mother
found it. She slapped me across the face and
put extra pepper in the next bowl. I eventually
turned to hiding the rice in my pants, then
flushing it down the toilet in the bathroom.

I don't think I ever had or ever will feel more
trapped in my life. I realized that I was
petrified at the thought of running away with
nowhere to go, yet sick at the thought of
having to stay in that house with my mother.

Chapter 3... Subtle Cries for Help

I will lift up mine eyes unto the hills, from whence cometh my help. My help cometh from the LORD, which made heaven and earth.

Psalm 121:1-2(KJV)

The phrase "it takes a village to raise a child" has been used by some of the most influential child advocates around the world, and although it seems cliché, it holds great truth. Having been raised in an environment that could have benefited greatly from the presence and watchful eyes of other caring adults, I strongly agree with child advocates. Though I didn't have a village, I did have grandparents whose short lived visits were the highlight of my early life.

Oh, how happy I was when my grandparents came to pick me up from school. I knew this always meant hugs, kisses, and actually being talked to. This time, as I jumped in the back seat, they asked how my school day had been and said my mother wasn't feeling well. She'd asked them to pick me up for her. "Yes!" I thought. I could care less why my mother wasn't picking me up, anything to get me to my grandparents house for a few hours would do.

"She always has a big appetite when she comes over", said my grandmother to my grandfather. Along with hugs and kisses, going over to my grandparent's house always meant getting to eat as much food as I could stomach! Nobody ever went hungry at their house. My grandmother would jokingly remark about how she couldn't understand for the life of her how I ate so much and still managed to stay so skinny; but she also never knew of the nights I drank water to get full. As I grew older I realized the lack of food in our house could be explained by the amount of money my mother spent on liquor.

I soon noticed we were driving the same direction my mother went to take me home. In an instant, my facial expression changed from sunshine to gloom and my head drooped into my chest. I realized I wasn't going to my grandparent's house at all...

Were my silent screams for help not loud enough for them to hear? Were they not unnerved by how hungry I was each time I had an opportunity to eat at their home? Didn't they know my mother spent the money on alcohol she could have been using to keep food in the house? Was the forced smile I wore as I exited their car enough to hide how quickly my joy faded the closer we drove to my house?

Behind the Smile

They had no idea how many nights I'd filled my belly with water to stop hunger pains, or how many beatings I'd endured.

We pulled into my driveway and I got out of the car, wearing the only smile I could muster as I made my way to our door and rang the bell. All too quickly my mother answered the door and I quickly went inside as she waved goodbye to her parents. There I was again, in the darkest place of my existence; home.

Chapter 4... Perversion

A false witness shall not be unpunished, and he that speaketh lies shall not escape.
Proverbs 19:5 (KJV)

I still remember my stolen innocence like it was yesterday. As though a neglectful, alcoholic mother wasn't a hellacious enough existence at my age; I soon became easy pickings for sexual abuse. It seemed that the same look that got me overlooked in the classroom also screamed that I was not looked after, and an easy prey for being violated.

Most incidences of sexual abuse against a child are perpetrated by close friends of the family, and my case was no different. Though unrelated, these family friends are often referred to as a child's aunt or uncle. This friend is someone the parent feels can be trusted around their young child. Still, my experience proves that a mother should never leave her son or daughter alone in the company of her male companion. Never...

"Do you know how pretty you are?" This was the statement I'd heard several times from the husband of my mother's close friend. They had small children about my age, so when my mother would visit I'd play in the bedroom with the other kids. One day however, my mother and her friend went shopping and left me to play with the children under the supervision of the husband.

He soon sent his children outside to play and asked me to stay behind. He offered me ice cream and asked me to sit next to him on the couch. As I ate my ice cream he stared at me with the strangest look in his eyes. He placed his hand on my thigh and told me again how pretty I was, and how brown my skin was. His smile quickly became more and more of a grimace, and I remember feeling so strange on the inside. I stared at the door; heart beating out of my chest, just hoping one of the other children would come inside and interrupt.

I think I may have eaten that ice cream cone in record time, and didn't hesitate to ask if I could go outside to join the other children. He agreed, but there was one condition… I had to give him a kiss on his cheek. Fearful and unsure of how'd I'd get away from him otherwise, I gave him a peck on the cheek and he allowed me to leave.

Without him aggressively attacking me, even as a child I knew something about this encounter made me very uncomfortable. I'd just had my first "bad touch" experience. With no one to explain what had happened, and no one paying close enough attention to protect me; this was just the beginning.

Later, that same man left his wife and children, and moved in with my mother and I. At first, everything was fine. It wasn't until my mother started working late when things took a turn for the worst. It wasn't long before I'd lost my virginity to my mother's boyfriend.
Everything I knew about sex I'd learned through my encounters with him. Sometimes he wouldn't touch me at all; he would masturbate in front of me or force my hand to hold his penis.
I often questioned how my mother could have never suspected anything. Don't mothers have this innate ability to just know when something is wrong with their babies?
Granted, my mother had a special hatred and detachment when it came to me, but how could she just not know? No stranger to feeling trapped, most days I simply endured it, pretending I was somewhere else, anywhere but underneath him…

My school years were even more horrible than before after the sexual abuse started. Of course my mother never encouraged me to participate in anything, so I had hardly any social skills and didn't get involved in anything going on at school. My hermit ways didn't make me the most popular girl, so I was often ridiculed by the other children for being ugly and skinny.

I never had a desire to do much of anything aside from staying in my room, watching TV, or listening to music. Music was my love. It was my escape from life. For four to seven minutes I'd be the person in the song, living a life I could only dream of. Music was an expression of the things I wished I could say, and all the things I'd never had the courage to do. Hiding away in my room to listen to music was about all I had the focus to do for long periods of time. I was so preoccupied with the stress of my home life that nothing in school kept me interested.

I was always on edge and still constantly suffering from stomach pains. I lived in constant stress and fear from day to day. Would this be a normal day? Would my mother's boyfriend bother me today? Some days he was normal; but other days he would look at me from across the room, and when my mother turned her back, he'd blow me a kiss or wiggle his tongue at me with that devilish smile. I knew that meant he would be visiting me in my room that night.

I started wearing clothes underneath my

pajamas to try to throw him off. I would see the hallway light come on and know that in a few moments he'd be at my door. I could always hear him coming because I could never sleep soundly in that house. Like clock work, he would come in very slowly and begin to rub my body. I'd pretend to be asleep, and in one swift motion, roll my body in a way that would not give him direct access to any of my private parts. He would continue until he felt the clothing I was wearing underneath my pajamas. Then he would leave. Whew! I'd made it through another night...

Not oblivious to my strategy for keeping him off of me, he'd usually retaliate the next day by getting me into trouble for something minor like not taking out the trash or leaving a dirty pot in the sink. Still, that was better than another night with him. After my mother would punish me for whatever he'd ratted me out for, he'd find me and say that if I would have let him do what he wanted the night before this would not be happening. "I know you aren't really sleeping anyway", he would say sarcastically. "If you tell, no one will believe you", he always assured me.

I did once work up the courage to tell my friend who lived next door. I was desperate and wanted it to stop. My friend told her mother, and I just knew my mother's boyfriend would get what he deserved once and for all, or that someone would come and finally get me out of there. Unfortunately, my friend's mother response was how horrible that was and advised me to tell the police! That was it! It failed almost as miserably as my attempt to run away from home… Starting to believe that he was right, either no one cared or no one would believe me, I never told again.

The abuse continued for several years after that, and so did my poor school performance and lack of interest. By this time my mother had stopped drinking for the most part, but that didn't make her much more pleasant to live with. Apparently, her boyfriend would allow her to drink occasionally, or so he said. "You will cause your mother to start drinking again", he would always say if I threatened to tell her about the sexual abuse. "I will lie and get you into trouble", was another one of his favorite threats.

Between my mothers's perverted boyfriend telling me I was pretty and my mother constantly screaming at me; I had no self esteem. I kept silent and stayed in my bedroom for the most part. My mother would make me come out of my room to watch the news and sometimes a game show. Jeopardy usually; for the educational value of coarse. I dreaded coming out of my room because that's when my mother's boyfriend would begin to stare at me. He'd glare at me with that devilish smirk each time she turned her back, and I'd try my best to pretend not to see him... But I always noticed.

Though I cannot remember exactly how old I was at the time, certainly in my early teens; I'll never forget missing my period. Pregnancy scare is an understatement; this would have qualified as a pregnancy disaster! Pregnant by my mother's boyfriend! In my mind it couldn't get any worse than that. I initially had not even realized I was late on my period, but my mother's boyfriend knew immediately. I remember him asking me if my period had started and I told him it hadn't. He told me I should have started because my mother had already had her period. Apparently, he had been monitoring my cycles like clockwork.

At about two weeks late, fear and panic gripped me. My mother's boyfriend assured me that everything would be okay. He said that if I was really pregnant he would take care of the baby. What a disaster! He told me to lie and say that some boy from school had gotten me pregnant. He promised that he would raise the child and that no one would ever know the truth. How could this be happening?! There was no way I could be pregnant by my mother's boyfriend. If it wasn't before, my life was officially over.

Four days later I got my life back when my period started, but soon realized my cycle was more in tune with my mothers than I imagined. She was the pregnant one!

I remember wondering why my mother wasn't at work the particular day I found out. My first thought was, "Oh no! She's started drinking again!" I walked into a quiet house, and my mother's bedroom door was closed. Just as I begin to suspect that no one was home, my mother's boyfriend came down the stairs and explained that she was home sick from a surgery she'd had that morning. I asked what kind of surgery, and he told me she had gotten her tubes tied. He then explained that she had also gotten pregnant and had an abortion.

I stood in the middle of the floor frozen. Her boyfriend went on explaining that she didn't want any children so she had her tubes tied. In spite of how badly she treated me, I couldn't believe my mother killed her baby. Somehow the abortion seemed to solidify just how much she must have hated and regretted having me. I remember it being a long time after that before I could even look my mother in her eyes again.

Chapter 5... Insanity

And the peace of God, which passeth all understanding, shall keep your hearts and minds through Christ Jesus.

Philippians 4:7 (KJV)

As hardened as my life must have made me, I did eventually reach a breaking point. For some people the breaking point is suicide, for me, it was attempting to stab my mother in her sleep. Of course everyone thought I'd gone nuts, but who could blame me?! My attempt to end my suffering failed, but not before it landed me in an inpatient psychiatric treatment facility for children. Forced to live with an abusive alcoholic mother and a child molester, and here I was under psychiatric observation in a wooden box!

Literally a wooden box, every piece of furniture in my room seemed to be made of light colored wood; the bed frame, the closet, the drawers, the night stand, all wood. Still today, I can't recall the name of the facility or how long I was there. What I do remember is how hush hush my entire family was about the entire ordeal. No one in my family talked about the incident, and my grandparents only came to visit me once during my entire stay at the center.

How did I get here? What was I thinking? Why did I pull that knife out of the kitchen drawer in the middle of the night? Maybe I was as crazy as everyone seemed to think I was. All I wanted to do was stop her from hitting me, and stop her boyfriend from touching me. I dreamed of going to live with my grandparents, thinking I'd be safe there... But that dream never became a reality. No one seemed to question why I'd not only attempted to run away once, but now I'd tried to kill my mother.

Instead of sympathy or concern, there I was in a small, cold wooden room, still alone. I was told to put my things in the closet and wait for someone to come get me. I remember it only taking me a few minutes to unpack, because my mother hadn't put much of anything in that little bag.

I don't remember taking any medication, but was required to talk to a therapist daily. She of course wanted to know why I tried to hurt my mother. I wanted to tell her the truth; that I was going to get another bashing because my grades were bad. I also wanted to explain that my grades were bad because my mother's boyfriend was doing bad things to me. But my mother's boyfriend had already warned me never to tell. He assured me that even if I did, my mother would never believe me, and that I would only get into more trouble for lying. So there I was, too afraid to speak. In fact, I never said a word. For hours I'd sit there, rubbing my hands together and crying; everyday the same routine.

I never told of the physical or sexual abuse I'd been enduring to anyone in the center. Oddly enough, my mother would even ask me why I refused to talk to the doctor. "Why doesn't she know what he's been doing to me?" I wondered. "Why won't she stop using me as a punching bag?" I'm sure I prolonged my stay at the center by refusing to talk at all. But the truth was that I was more petrified at the thought of going back home than the thought of ending up in that wooden box forever.

Chapter 6... Enough Is Enough

And from the days of John the Baptist until now the kingdom of heaven suffers violence, and the violent take it by force.

Matthew 11:12 (NKJV)

After all my years of suffering in silence, believe it or not, the Oprah Winfrey show inspired me to finally speak out about the many years of abuse I'd experienced. I remember watching an episode and hearing Oprah say with boldness the key to my freedom. She stated that the abuse would never stop until a person confronted their abuser and exposed them for who they were. So from that moment forward, I looked for my opportunity to come clean.

One day, while at my aunt's house, my cousin and I decided to play Wiji board. I had heard stories about the game being a fake; but I thought I would try it anyway. My cousin started by asking the board a question and it spelled out an answer. She said it was right so we played on. All of a sudden, my cousin asked if anyone had ever hurt me. I looked at her and the board answered yes. Then she asked if it was someone she knew, and again, the board answered yes. She then asked if it was still happening, and again, the board answered yes.

With tears dropping from my eyes, I looked at my cousin and my aunt, and before I knew what was happening I was telling them everything. My aunt said that she had known something wasn't right but could never put her finger on exactly what was going on. She couldn't believe I suffered all those years and didn't tell anyone. I told her that I was afraid my mother would start drinking again or wouldn't believe me. She said that I could stay with her until everything was sorted out.

I remember feeling like a million dollars! Oprah was right! Finally, I would be free from my abuser! As I sat on the couch that would later become my bed for a while, I kept thinking about how unbelievable it was that this day had finally arrived.

I wish I could say things went smoothly from here, but they didn't. It didn't take long for my aunt to sell me out. Well, at least that's what I called it. Her attitude toward me gradually started to change. She said my mother thought I was making it all up! I was distraught. How could she believe that after I trusted her? Once again, an attempt at freedom had ended in me being the bad guy. In another unreal experience, I was reliving years past; and once again, everyone was looking at me like I was crazy and needed to go back to the inpatient psych treatment center. After only a few days on the couch, I was forced to return home.

My mother was upset and crying when I returned. Apparently, her boyfriend had confessed before I got there. Still, in another sick twist, as though I'd not suffered long enough; my mother explained that he'd have nowhere to go if she kicked him out, but wanted me to ultimately decide what I was comfortable with. Why would a parent force the victim to choose the fate of the perpetrator? Why did she care about him having somewhere to go, but didn't seem so bothered by the idea of him remaining in the house with the daughter he'd been raping?!

She said he would stay in the spare bedroom if that was ok, but she left the entire decision making process up to me. She said that if I wanted to press charges against her boyfriend it was optional. She also made it clear that telling my grandparents would hurt them, but said that was my choice as well. I could not believe her! My mother hated me, but this was sick, even for her. I really didn't care at that point how she felt about me. I was just tired of being on edge. Parents are supposed to protect and love their children, not hurt and abuse them or stand by while it happens.

That house had officially become unlivable. I was the evil one, and my mother and her boyfriend both made that very clear. No one talked, we simply co-existed. My mother stayed in her bedroom, crying and drinking. Her boyfriend stayed in the spare bedroom, and I hardly ever left the basement. I tried to stay away from home as much as possible, and when I finally couldn't take it any longer, I asked my boyfriend if he thought his mother would allow me to move in with them. He asked, and after I told her some of my story, she agreed.

Chapter 7... From Bad to Bad

But may the God of all grace, who called us to His eternal glory by Christ Jesus, after you have suffered a while, perfect, establish, strengthen, and settle you.
I Peter 5:10 (KJV)

Sex meant nothing to me by the time I was living with my boyfriend. If he asked for it, I would do it. I didn't even know I'd developed a reputation for being easy. To me, it was no big deal. Moving in with my boyfriend, who later became my husband, was my quick fix. I was so happy that he still wanted to be with me in spite of my past. What I didn't realize at the time was that he was just as messed up as I was. Still, with a skewed perception of love and sex, it didn't take long for me to end up pregnant.

Hurting people hurt other people, and dysfunction can only breed dysfunction because that is all the person knows. I can't say that my time living with my husband's family was good, it was just a fix. Shortly after we found out I was pregnant I moved back in with my mother, who by that time had totally kicked her boyfriend out. Things were still very tense between us. She was very angry when we told her I was pregnant, and she wanted to know what I was going to do about the pregnancy. I told her I planned to keep my baby; of course, we'd already established that I didn't agree with abortion. My mother kept saying how disappointed she was, but I didn't care. How could she criticize me for something I had done? Look at what she allowed to happen to me for eight years!

After the baby was born, my boyfriend and I decided to get married; and although we had many years of bumps and bruises, we had a total of three wonderful boys and loved them dearly. Meanwhile, my mother spiraled out of control with her drinking and depression, and eventually had to be put in a rehab center. Once she completed her program she moved away with her parents.

My marriage was going down faster than a sinking ship, and once again, I felt alone and stressed. A friend at work had been trying for months to get me to come to church with her. She would often find me crying in the bathroom or see me walking around with my head down. I eventually couldn't take it anymore. I was so tired of arguing and fighting with my husband, I would have agreed to do anything I thought would help. I agreed to go to church with her and ending up giving my life to Christ.

I felt like the whole world was lifted off of my shoulders that day. I couldn't believe how easy it was! I was so excited that I rushed home to tell my husband. His reaction was far from what I'd expected though. He got upset and accused me of thinking I was better than him because I'd given my life to Christ! I couldn't believe what I was hearing! He was actually mad at me for confessing Christ, and not two weeks later I came home from work to find my husband moving out of the house.

He said he'd had enough. Not only did he leave me, but he left me and the children with no food in the house. I was totally caught off guard. This was nothing like what I'd imagined. It wasn't supposed to be this way! "Is this what happens when you give your life to Christ?!" I wondered. Still, though I couldn't see it at the time, him leaving would later prove to be a blessing...

Though I'd move away, it's hard to run from a failing marriage and a person you're connected to by three children. Where do you find rest when the one place on earth that should always be a safe haven is chaotic and hellacious? How many work and church activities do you have to bury yourself in to steal away from an enemy you share a bed with? We walk past men and women whose marriages and families are falling apart everyday. Each week we sit in pews next to men and women being abused by their spouses. While they may never open up and share the intimate details of their lives with you, behind the smiles they wear to keep you from being uncomfortable or discovering the truth, a compassionate friend may be just what they need. There's nothing worse than being alone in one of the loneliest places on earth; facing divorce.

Now separated from my husband, and taking care of two small children, I felt so abandoned. Confusion seemed to consume my mind as I struggled to pin point what exactly had gone so terribly wrong. My desire wasn't far fetched; or was it? All I wanted was to have a family, and to live happily ever after with my husband; in spite of having no concept of what a healthy family unit even looked like. I held on to my belief that marriage was wonderful, and having children together was just what people did. Unfortunately, I was the only person with such hopeful enthusiasm... On the other hand, the pressures of raising children, having a wife, and never maintaining a job were just too much for my husband to bear.

Desperately pursuing the remedy of an empty life and marriage, I was diligently trying to find myself through my relationship with God and became more and more active in the church. My husband and I tried several times to salvage our relationship, but there was simply too much resentment and disappointment built up between the two of us. Oddly, the same resentment and disappointment that was destroying my marriage didn't completely destroy our sex life. Before long, I discovered I was pregnant again. Needless to say, this time it was not a joyous occasion. My husband had no desire for another child, and to make matters worse, I was already living on the other side of town struggling with the sons we had. The word around town was that he'd already moved on, and I couldn't be surprised; fidelity had never been my husband's strong suit.

For the first time in our relationship my husband looked at me with disgust, as if I was his enemy. It was as though he actually believed I was to blame for becoming pregnant. We barely spoke to one another accept for when he wanted to see the children, or when I was arguing with him about helping me financially support them.

To make matters worse, about halfway through the pregnancy my mother came for a visit. Once I told her I was pregnant she simply asked, "What are you going to do with another kid?" Maybe a part of the little girl inside of me expected more than that for a change. My response was frank, "The same thing I've done with the others; raise it." My mother knew this time, unlike before, that was the end of the discussion.

Separated from my husband with very little financial support, I'd asked my childhood friend if she would move in with me and share the expenses; she agreed. I thought this agreement would also finally mean having some company; but I couldn't have been more wrong. I worked days, she worked nights, and we barely saw each other on the weekends.

By now I was going to church as much as possible in an attempt to stay focused. Still, I often found myself screaming with pain into my pillow in the middle of the night, being careful not to wake the children on the other side of the wall. At such a young age, the reality had set it that I'd managed to make a huge mess of my life. I couldn't figure out why my every attempt at happiness or normalcy seemed to end in disarray, and at that point, I had no idea how to undo the mess I'd made.

I was officially walking through one of the loneliness periods of my life; struggling to provide for myself and my children, without a friend, family, or the one person that had vowed to stay with me forever.

Chapter 8...The Straw That Broke the Camel

For we do not wrestle against flesh and blood, but against principalities, against powers, against the rulers of the darkness of this age, against spiritual host of wickedness in the heavenly places.

Ephesians 6:12 (NKJV)

I woke up to what seemed to have become my new norm. Work was stressful and home life wasn't much better. This particular day my husband had asked if I'd bring the children to his mother's house to visit him. When we arrived, I let him know that the children hadn't eaten yet. He asked me to drive to a nearby Wendy's so that he could buy them something to eat.

As we were sitting in the drive through, our children strapped in behind us, he began to look at me with such rage. I asked him what was wrong, and he responded that I made him sick. I immediately became angry at him for making such a statement in front of our children, and told him I didn't want to do this with them in the back seat. Still, he continued. Ranting and raving about how I thought everything was about me, and how he hated me for taking his kids away from him. I told him that I had not taken his children away from him, and reminded him that he never checked on them or gave me any money in an attempt to ensure that they were even provided for. His rage continued to grow as he questioned why I'd blocked him from picking the children up from daycare. I gave him the most honest answer I could muster, I didn't trust him. He went on yelling about how they were his children too and that he had rights that I couldn't just take away from him.

After what seemed to be the longest car ride I'd ever endured, we finally arrived back at his mother's house and got the children inside. Our arguing continued outside as he threatened that he wouldn't allow me to get away with my actions. It amazed me that the man that had abandoned us, leaving me to get by with little to no help from him, was now feeling somehow victimized by me. It was clear that our words war was headed nowhere fast, and I'd heard enough.

Fed up, I told him that I'd bring the children back when he calmed down. I made my way toward this house to gather the children when he began yelling, "you're not taking them from me!" He stood in front of the door, his figure like a looming wall between me and my children, and his words like piercing arrows being shot from keepers of a gate under siege. I yelled for him to move, and attempted to reason with him; assuring him that I'd bring the children back when he calmed down. Unmovable, he quickly responded no, saying that I could leave but that the boys were staying with their father.

As I attempted to get one of the boys out of the front door, his mother stood by holding our youngest son. As though it were stripped from the pages of an award winning Hollywood drama, in what felt like only a flash of a second, my husband had grabbed our son out of my arms, sat him down, and pushed me onto the couch. Now in survival mode, in response to a position of abuse I was not unfamiliar with, I attempted to quickly jump to my feet. He grabbed both my arms and pushed again as I stumbled backward trying to catch myself. I kept yelling over and over again, "I am not leaving without my children!"

By this time both boys were crying and screaming at the sight of their mother telling their father to stop and let me go. My husband then grabbed me and through me back on the couch, this time jumping on top of me with a couch pillow and placing it over my face. He pressed with such force that in an instant I recall thinking, "I am going to die today."

The funny thing is that in the midst of all I'd been through, the thought of death was one of peace instead of fear. Perhaps it was the cries of my young children in the background that awakened the fight buried inside of me, underneath years of pain and exhaustion. If I wasn't motivated to keep living for me, I refused to abandon them the way I'd felt abandoned my entire life. So I fought.

As I struggled to get free, his mother yelled at him to stop and started pulling on his shirt until he finally got off of me. As I lay there catching my breath, he continued to yell how much he hated me, and that they were his children too. He finally let the boys and I leave. I was eight months pregnant...

As I got back into the car, I knew my husband and I had crossed a line we couldn't step back over, and what once was, was now shattered into pieces that could never be mended. At that moment I was officially scared of the man that I had committed my life to, the man I'd run to for refuge from a horrible childhood filled with abuse. For the first time since we'd met, I finally faced the realization that my husband was just as messed up in the head as I was; and I knew that we'd never be good for one another again.

Chapter 9...Anywhere But Here

The Lord also will be a refuge for the oppressed, a refuge in times of trouble.

Psalms 9:9(NKJV)

Exhausted and still crying from the horrific ordeal with my husband earlier that day; I put the children to bed and lay down. Sobbing on and off throughout most of the night; I eventually fell asleep, only to be woken up by throbbing pain in my left foot. Hardly able to stand, I looked down to find my ankle solid black and swollen. I limped toward the kitchen for an ice pack as my mind ran hurdles considering believable excuses I could give my boss for why I'd clearly not be going in to work.

I called my boss, and by the time I finished explaining that at 8 months pregnant I'd slipped on my kitchen floor, she insisted that I go see a doctor instead of reporting for my shift. There was no way I could tell her that I had a horrible fight with my husband who pushed me around like a rag doll then attempted to kill me by suffocation. Unfortunately, after going to the doctor it was confirmed that my ankle was indeed broken. I was placed in a walking cast because of my pregnancy, and was taken off of work and now stuck at home to constantly relive one of the scariest events I'd ever experienced.

My husband called, but only to start another argument. I told him that I had broken my ankle and was in a cast. He said it was my fault and that I deserved it. That was it. No more tears. No more yelling. No more doubt. At that very moment I knew I could not continue being in the marriage, and I definitely was not going to fight with him over our children. I decided to run. But where would I go? My family was in another state.

I eventually spoke candidly with my boss about what had been going on when I turned in my disability papers. It came as no surprise to her as she already knew I wasn't telling the truth about slipping on my kitchen floor. As I cried uncontrollably she told me I had to leave for my safety and the safety of the children. So with nowhere else to turn, I did something that I thought I would never do again. I asked for help from the one person who'd abandoned me and proved unreliable for most of my life. A person who'd chosen her daughter's abuser over the very child she gave birth to.

That night after talking to my boss, I called my mother. I explained what had happened, and much to my surprise she didn't seem too upset.

I told her I needed to leave the state, and asked if the boys and I could stay with her and my grandparents. After a long and awkward pause, she said she wasn't sure; that'd she would ask and call me back. I was livid! Once again, my heart longed for a reaction that would reveal some sort of compassion from a mother heartbroken to learn that her daughter had been the victim of domestic violence.

I ached with expectation of sympathy from a mother whose daughter was fighting for her safety and in a marriage that was in the toilet. I just wanted this to be the time I was met by a voice of love and concern. My desire to still be rescued by my mother even as a grown woman was shattered in an instant as reality set in and all I got was a dry "I'll call you back".

The return call came, followed by some travel money via Western Union. And before I knew it I had packed everything I could fit into my Ford Taurus. With children in the back seat, my leg in a cast, and a bassinet in the passenger seat; I hit the road in the middle of the night and never looked back.

Chapter 10...Home Sweet Home

So now we can rejoice in our wonderful new relationship with God because our Lord Jesus Christ has made us friends of God.

Romans 5:11 (NLT)

Living with your family can sometimes be considered either a curse or a blessing... I suppose, once I got over the initial embarrassment of it all, I was comfortable. It was a wonderful opportunity for my mother and the rest of our family to enjoy the grandchildren and new baby. Still, I longed to find a church so that I could reconnect to the things of God. I visited several churches with no success.

Oddly enough, it was the money I'd been collecting for my leg injury running out that opened the door for me to find what I'd so desperately been searching for. I was able to find a part-time job teaching at a career college, and one evening I over heard a student saying that Bishop T.D. Jakes was coming to her church. I of course immediately wanted to know what church she went to. She told me she attended Harvest Church and invited me to go. What an answer to my prayers! I was so tired of going from church to church, and I was excited to visit this one.

I showed up that Sunday and heard Pastor Steve Houpe ministering with a strength I'd not encountered anywhere else, and I knew I was home.

As I joined one house, the house I shared with my mother seemed to be getting smaller by the minute. Still, things were working out surprisingly well between my family and I. I eventually found a full-time job and moved out of my mother's house into an apartment, much to my relief. As the boys and I settled in, I continued to attend church, and after a few short months met another single mother. We immediately became friends. Friendship may be common place for someone that doesn't share my testimony, but because I'd spent most of my life feeling alone, her friendship was a blessing. We couldn't explain it, but we knew God knit our hearts together; and over the next several years, I became a part of her family.

Her family showed me and my children more love then we had experienced in a long time and as I continued to grow in the Word of God. He began to show me that all people are not abusive, angry, violent, or liars. She and I used each other as encouragement and made a commitment that we would stick by each other no matter what. We stumbled together, laughed together, cried together, and grew in the things of God together. God knows what you need and who you need just at the right time. God uses people to fill the gaps. I never knew a family you don't even belong to could take you in, love you, and support you. It was a love I desperately needed at that time in my life.

The relationship between my mother and I was civil. She was instrumental in watching the boys for me after I decided to return to school and pursue my dreams of becoming an early childhood education teacher. Although it was still an obvious struggle, I was committed to trying to make the best out of an awkward relationship.

As time progressed I was doing well in school, I had a wonderful job in the medical field and was very active in the church. In my mind however, the struggles were still present. The feeling that I had failed my children as a mother by not staying with their father hung over my head like an anvil. I was divorced; which carries such a negative tone with three children. "No man in his right mind would want to marry me for sure", I thought. I'd convinced myself that I was doomed to remain single, at least until my children grew up.

I had no understanding that everything is done in Gods timing. His timing is perfect because He knows everything that you need and when you need it. Although we have great desires, many things we pray for can not come until we have settled some issues and developed certain characteristics that will be necessary to move into those next stages of our lives. You see, God's will is for us to be strong in our body, mind, and spirit. And because He is God, He will settle for nothing less then complete and total restoration of a broken person. That's what I was; a broken person who had tried many times over the course of my life to fix those broken areas with band-aides. Later, only to have the band-aides wear and fall off to expose the shattered image I maintained of myself. I'd bandaged brokenness and written off my deepest scars as hopeless.

As much as God wanted to heal my broken life, I first had to acknowledge the brokenness, forgive anyone who assisted in the breakage, and move forward. Though the mess of a life I'd live seemed almost an impossible task to restore in my mind; my desire to be healed was stronger than any of my doubts. So I made the choice to forgive, and allowed God's process to officially begin.

Chapter 11... Forgiveness & Restoration

But if you do not forgive men their trespasses, neither will your Father forgive your trespasses.
                                                        Matthew 6:15 (NKJV)

It wasn't long before all the extra time I was spending at church and in the Word to combat my loneliness started to pay off. I learned who I was in Christ for the first time. I was not the person people from my past told me I was. I was not to blame for all those years of physical and emotional abuse. I learned how to confront my past, and most importantly, I learned how to forgive and move forward. Forgiveness was the key if I was going to live a life of peace; and I had to face the fact that suppression of what had happened to me was not the same as forgiveness.

Forgiveness, is releasing the person or persons who have harmed you, whether in person or in spirit, and moving forward. Forgiveness is being able to pray for the deliverance of the very people that once harmed you, and mean it from your heart. Forgiveness is being able to bless those that have wronged you, through both prayer and good deeds.

In order to forgive a person who has harmed you, you first must understand that it was part of the plan. Ok, let me clarify this statement. You see, God had a divine plan for your life before you were created. We are the ones who change the path through the decisions that we make along the way. When you look back and evaluate your life, I'm sure you can take note of events that have changed who you are as a person. And those experiences that affected you so greatly caused you to change course. We are the sum total of our experiences.

God is everything that represents love, peace, joy and life. However, life happens and bad things happen to good people. What Father God does is take those experiences and turn them around for your benefit. My mother's alcoholism stole my childhood; my sexual abuse at the hand of her boyfriend stole my innocence and sense of security. Yet, my mother's alcoholism made me strong and independent, my sexual abuse at the hand of her boyfriend made me sensitive to other hurting children in need of love and security from an adult.

My childhood caused me many years of pain and shame as an adult. Still, God's Word taught me to trust only in Him and to love and forgive those who cause pain. To understand that the abuse wasn't my fault and that I am important and very much needed in the

Kingdom of God. God taught me to love a person in spite of their short comings. It was this healing journey that set me on the path to reconnecting with a father that'd been absent my entire life.

"I don't know whether he is dead or alive", was always my response if anyone asked me about my father. That was the truth. I had lost contact with my father. I saw him for the last time when I was about seventeen, and our encounter wasn't a very good one. This was right after my life was crashing around me and I was exposing all the abuse that I had endured. I was angry at him because he wasn't there. He never checked on me to see if I was ok. He just lived his life as if I didn't even exist.

I realize now that it was a pointless conversation because he had no clue what I was talking about. He had no idea what I had gone through during my childhood and at that time I was still harboring too many emotions to communicate very effectively. We parted ways for what would be fifteen years of silence after that.

Little did I know that God was going to restore what the enemy had tried to devour. After sitting through one of the most profound sermons by my pastor on forgiveness, God revealed it was time for me to forgive my father for not being in my life. Pastor said, "True healing can't begin until you completely and totally give all your hurt, pain, disappointment, anger, and heart ache to God". So, after the service I decided to seek out my father.

I remember it like it was just yesterday. It was in December, with both of our birthday fast approaching come January. I went online and did a Google search by his name; and just like that, there he was. I was nervous at first because I knew that once I opened the file with his information, I'd no longer be able to claim I didn't know whether or not my father was dead or alive. Determined to move forward, I paid the fee and within minutes I had his last known address.

I got the idea to send him a birthday card. On the inside I wrote him a hello note with my phone number. I wasn't sure if he would call me but what I did know is I had done what God told me to do. Within a week or so, I received a call and heard a voice that I hadn't heard in fifteen years. It was strange yet exciting to see God move so quickly after my simple obedience. Over the course of several months I would be reunited with family; some

Behind the Smile

I was just meeting for the first time and some I had not seen since I was a little girl. God restored time as if it had never slipped away.

Chapter 12... New Beginnings

This means that anyone who belongs to Christ has become a new person. The old life is gone; a new life has begun!

2 Corinthians 5:17 (NLT)

A time of healing comes to all who desire it. Once you've decided that enough is enough; surrender completely to God's plan for your life. Then, and only then, can you truly begin to heal wounds that originate deep within your soul. That's exactly what I did. Through the biblical teachings of my pastor Dr. Steve Houpe, and his wife Dr. Donna Houpe, I was truly able to understand the healing power of God.

Who would have thought I'd be in this place all these years later, a place of victory? Certainly, not me. It seemed as though this day would never come while I spent most of my life so desperate for love that I'd believe anyone who said those three words. When they hurt me, abused me, neglected me; I just ignored it and counted it all as love. I used to refer to myself as the faithful little puppy that always came back for more.

So many times we find ourselves disappointed by family members and friends because we set unrealistic expectations for them. Simply put, we are looking for an unconditional love that only God himself can give. Many of us sell our very souls chasing that love; a love that can never be bought.

I finally knew I served a God that says He's loved me before the foundation of the world, and had proven it through His sacrifice. His love comes with no conditions or strings attached. His love is not predicated on my performance. Once I accepted His son as Lord of my life, it was finished.

Why me Lord? Why did I have to be abused? Yes, I asked God why. Many people say we shouldn't question God concerning why things happen. That doesn't make sense to me. I'm asking the person who allowed those things to happen. However, what I've learned through the Word of God is that the question is not why, but how. How can I take these events and use them to point people to Christ? How can I forgive and then encourage another person? You see, we all experience storms, trials, and tribulations. The key is to go "through" them, not wallow in them.

Once I overcame the embarrassment of what I'd experienced, I realized that I must tell my story to others who are going "through" as well. I must tell of the abuse, the failed marriage, and raising three children on my own. I must tell of starting my life over in a new state, and tell of holding on to the hand of God with every fiber of my being. I must tell of the struggle to keep my sanity and to not roll over and die. Yes, die, as I considered death on many occasions. I spent many years in silent suffering, but today, I must share that just when I thought life was unbearable and I couldn't take another step; God came in and breathed on me the breath of life, and He restored my strength so that I could see this new day.

No more woe is me, no more playing the victim or making excuses as to why I couldn't make it over the hump toward success in life. I made a decision, for the sake of my children, that I would offer them something more than excuses. I wanted them to have something I never experienced; a safe and secure home environment where God is honored and peace is evident. This would require me to totally surrender my life to God, and to believe that He desired something better for my life and the lives of my children than what we'd experienced. I had to choose to believe that I was born for a purpose, in spite of my beginnings.

Chapter 13...The Good Fight

Fight the good fight of faith, lay hold on eternal life, to which you were also called and have confessed the good confession in the presence of many witnesses.

I Timothy 6:12 (NKJV)

Consistent with boxing and other forms of physical combat, fighters have unique styles, stances, and defense techniques. This continues to hold true in many of life's battle arenas. For example, the stance some choose to prepare for a financial blow is worry, while others cling to savings accounts and economy watching. Some throw punches through faith and the power of confession, while others end up becoming their own greatest opponent through words of doubt and failure. Have you overlooked or misjudged someone in a fight? Sometimes that person that walks by without much to say isn't unkind; they're simply bogged down with life. Others hide behind the same half smile and casual, "I'm doing great" to camouflage the scrapes and bruises of a raging battle. Are you in a fight? Are you winning the battle? What determines whether a fight is good or bad is your faith.

Have you ever heard the expression "what doesn't kill us makes us stronger"? Well, that sums up the story of my life. I have always wondered why my life seemed so hard. Nothing ever seemed to just come easy to me. As diligent as I was, it always seemed that I had to work much harder than most people for anything I needed or wanted. It took great maturity for me to eventually come to the realization that God strengthens us through trials and tribulation. Needless to say, my life has consisted of many of both. I never could have dreamed that my lack of adequate amounts of food during childhood would prepare me for the lack I'd experience for a season raising three children on my own.

I never imaged how hard I would struggle, even after surrendering my life to Christ. The road didn't get better; in fact things started getting more difficult. It seemed as if every time I turned around I had issues on the job, and my money never seemed to add up to enough to cover all the bills at the end of the month. I literally lived from day to day sometimes not knowing how I was going to feed the children that evening. I often prayed that there would be free lunch at work so I would have something to eat myself.

I cried a lot of nights, had stomach ulcers and felt as if God had abandoned me and my children. Yet some how I mustard up the energy to get up everyday and keep moving. I didn't know where I was going or how I was going to get there. But I knew I had a helper; an unseen helper that in spite of what it looked like, and it often looked bad, was helping me take each step. Somehow, I'd drawn unimaginable strength from a past that may have killed someone else, and if I could fight through the years of abuse and abandonment, surely I could fight the fight of faith with my God who'd promised to never leave me.

One of my first true learning experiences was trusting God to take care of me and the children. This may sound easy, but relinquishing what I felt like was a burden that should naturally fall on me as a mother to God was one of the hardest acts of faith I'd ever encountered. I had to trust God with my life, safety, needs, and money. One of the main reasons this was such a difficult area to exercise faith in for me is because with my natural eyes, lack seemed to be the only thing I saw all around me. Still, I had to take God at his Word daily. Needless to say, some days were less than successful, and I found myself crying out to God, desperately desiring to know why my life felt so hard.

In the midst of fighting, I needed practical information, and lots of it. I needed survival skills and courage to believe my life could be better; and that it *would* be better than it was. I needed my children to not be afraid of life's adversities and difficulties, and to see their mother succeed in spite of all we'd been through. I needed role models and people who had walked in my shoes. I needed money, and lots of it! And so I turned to the only resource I knew, the Word of God.

I learned how to make it each day, standing on Faith. Faith is hope, and having hope generates strength, and having strength develops courage, and courage moves you to perseverance. Once faith, hope, strength, courage, and perseverance set in; you look up one day and realize that somehow you've arrived in a better place, and you made it through what seemed to be an impossible situation…

Chapter 14...Out Jumps The Bride!

He who finds a wife finds what is good and receives favor from the Lord.
                                        Proverbs 18:22 (NIV)

Marriages, and the desire to be married, are not only natural, but God given. Marriage was designed by God, like all good and perfect gifts, to be a fully functioning institution between one whole man and one whole woman. However, what happens when one or both of those people is broken? The reality is that God spends a lifetime mending our broken pieces and healing hurts that sometimes date back generations. This means that both inside and outside of the church, people are dating and marrying everyday with "issues". God made it clear that our issues don't disqualify us from His gifts when Jesus died while we were still in our sin. Still, while our issues don't disqualify us, they do shape our decisions, our perception, and the people we are behind the beautiful smiles that silently speak volumes to the opposite sex...

After years of singleness I felt I was ready to jump back in the saddle of marriage. My children had gotten older, and though I was still struggling financially, I had experienced tremendous growth spiritually. I'd dealt with understanding why my first marriage failed; and for the first time in my life, I had a clear sense of who I was and my self-esteem was at an all time high. After all we'd been through as a family, I felt it fitting to sit my children down at the kitchen table and share my desire to be married again with them. First there was silence, and then one by one they each gave their opinions. The general consensus was that they were all happy about the idea and in agreement. So we prayed that God would send me a husband…

Some time had passed and I'd decided to have some work done on my house. Much to my surprise, the man for the job turned out to be quite handsome, and it was clear that I'd caught his attention. A few weeks into working on my house, the man asked me to dinner. I said yes, and we had a refreshingly great time. So, he asked me out a second time and we had even more fun! Our conversations were wonderful, I asked all the "right" questions and he gave all the "right" answers. I was excited to be in a new relationship, and he shared my enthusiasm.

I just knew he was the "one"! He met my family; they loved him. I met his family; they loved me. After the hell I'd experienced, our relationship seemed near to perfection. As time went on, our relationship progressed, and we grew more and more comfortable with one another. He would attend church with me on occasion. He supported my children at basketball games. I supported him at his company by answering phones and organizing business files. It all seemed to be coming together so perfectly. After all the wrong, what a joy it was to finally have a sense of what right felt like; at least I thought…

It was a cold evening and the entire house was settling in for the night. My phone rang and there was a woman's voice on the other end. She verified my name at which time I replied yes. I knew she wasn't a bill collector or solicitor because it was too late in the evening for such a call. The woman on the other end of the phone proceeded to tell me that the man I had been involved with for months, the man that had shared holiday dinner with my family, the man that had attended church services with me, the man who'd cheered for my son during sports events; that man was married.

I didn't believe her. I couldn't believe her! I'd asked him if he was married the first day we exchanged numbers! His reply was a simple, "no". She went on to say that they had been separated for months, but that they were still married and I was committing sin by being with him. The thoughts in my head were swirling in a whirlwind of mixed emotion. I couldn't even muster the clarity of thought to respond to all of the accusations the wife of the man I was sure was my future husband was throwing at me through the phone. I finally gave up on the conversation all together, and simply said, "thank you for calling", then hung up the phone.

Stunned beyond belief, a huge flood of emotions began to flow from the pit of my stomach. This couldn't be happening to me! I did all the right things, and I asked all the right questions! He even gave all the right answers! Or so I thought... I needed support, and I needed it fast. I called my best friend and somehow spit out the words, "Help! Come over now!"

My best friend arrived shortly after my brief cry for help, and all I could manage to come up for air long enough to say through my sobbing was "he's married!" She stood stunned and wide eyed. She comforted me for hours as I retold the phone conversation over and over again. For days I walked in a state of shock, trying my best to put on a brave face in front of my children and the people around me. I wanted to call him and yell, curse, cry, and accuse; but I didn't.

A few days later, the phone rang, and it was him; speaking in a low voice as though he himself was in a state of mourning. I was surprised that he even had the nerve to call! He asked how I was doing and told me how sorry he was for everything. He went on to explain that he considered himself single and he was in the process of filing divorce papers. Excuses! I wanted no part of them. I yelled, cursed, cried, and he listened. He apologized again and said he wouldn't call anymore.

As I sat on the edge of my bed staring at the phone on its receiver, all I could do was wonder how I got to this place. I thought I had been so careful to follow the Word of God, and to do things the "right" way concerning my relationship. Yet here I was with my heart broken into little pieces, kicking myself because I felt I should have known. Why didn't I know? Were there signs that I ignored? Isn't God supposed to warn you of these things? Did He warn me and I ignored it?

Several months had past, and though I was getting better, I still wasn't over him. I replayed every detail of our relationship and how it ended over and over again in my head.

Behind the Smile

Though it can be productive to reflect on situations for the purpose of growth and understanding that was not what I was doing. I was allowing those thoughts to torment me, and ultimately, I was allowing them to stop me from moving forward. I blamed myself. I was embarrassed and ashamed...

Chapter 15...Around We Go

In your relationships with one another, have the same mindset as Christ Jesus.

Philippians 2:5 (NIV)

It was winter and my furnace had gone out one evening. I didn't know who to call. As I had the children put on extra clothing my ex popped into my head. Perhaps the thought itself was a setup, but my children were cold and he was the only person I knew personally with a maintenance business. I reasoned that it didn't have to be him that responded; maybe he could send one of his partners out to fix the furnace. After some brief deliberation in my mind, I made the phone call to the business line. I left a message on the recorder, careful to keep the call professional, I was very clear about my needs. I hung up and hoped I would get a call back before the cold of night set in.

Later that evening the callback had still not come. Suddenly the doorbell rang. I opened the front door and much to my surprise, there he stood. He looked sad and kind of sickly. His son who often worked with him on weekends stood there as well. We shared a brief stare and I let them in. They both walked straight downstairs without a word of conversation. My furnace was fixed within minutes, and he instructed his son to reload the tools in the truck.

We stared at each other awkwardly for several more minutes. I asked him what I owed him for the job. He said I didn't have to pay him anything and that he missed me. He also informed me that he had filed his divorce papers and was waiting on a court date. I told him I was sorry to hear that. He responded quickly, "Don't be", and asked if he could call sometime. I said yes and he left.

A week later we began talking on the phone again. Two weeks later we had dinner and the relationship was rekindled. Several months in I arrived home from work to hear the phone ringing. It was him on the other end asking if he could stop by for a few minutes. I agreed. The doorbell rang less then five minutes later, and he entered, greeting me with the strangest look on his face. He then proceeded to get on one knee and propose with a beautiful diamond solitaire.

I couldn't believe this was finally happening! What I had dreamed, fussed, yelled, and cried about for the past two years was finally taking place! My children were beaming with joy! Apparently, they already knew he was going to propose and even helped him select the ring.

I said yes and it seemed my whole world changed for the better in an instant.

He took everyone to dinner that night to celebrate our engagement. While in the restaurant, as I gazed at the ring on my finger I felt a huge weight in the pit of my stomach. I stared at my plate of food and couldn't eat. That was God's sign, but I ignored it and wrote it off as excitement.

Preparation followed and within a matter of months we had a wedding planned and paid for. Then one day out of the blue, I could not reach him by phone. I drove over to his house to find him not there. I called and called and kept getting his voicemail. My heart began to pound, and my emotions were off the chart. What is going on? We were only 30 days away from our wedding day after all we'd been through and I couldn't reach him! Then finally, he answered; but only to state that he needed some time to think and would call me later.

"Later" turned into the next day and the words that no bride-to-be ever wants to hear were spoken. "I don't think we should get married". I was devastated, confused, embarrassed and unable to breathe! He told me the Lord showed him what my life would be like if we married, and that it was not good. He said he refused to destroy my purpose and destiny, and as much as it hurt him and would hurt me, he had to call off the wedding. What could I say? How can you argue with a man who believes he heard from God?

As I healed from the loss, over time God slowly revealed to me why our marriage would not have worked. Though we often override warning signals and wrong way signs; God is so committed to you, that even when you can't see the truth, He steps in to save you. I am so grateful that God's love stretches far beyond our human capacity to reason or comprehend. With this revelation, I couldn't wallow in my circumstances. I made the decision to keep moving forward, to keep fighting, and to keep believing God's promises for my life; after all, it's faith that had gotten me this far.

Chapter 16...Nowhere to Hide

The instructions of the Lord are perfect, reviving the soul. The decrees of the Lord are trustworthy, making wise the simple.

Psalms 19:7 (NLT)

It was the November 2010 women's weekend encounter at church, and I'd just been terminated a month prior from what seemed like the best job I'd ever had. Teaching made me feel fulfilled, like motherhood, and now I was empty. I'd been fighting most of my life, and I wasn't quite sure I had anything left. Little did I know my emptiness was a setup for the most fulfilling encounter with God I'd ever had.

I found myself in the encounter not sure what to pray or ask for. Of course I didn't have a job, but that wasn't my concern; I was just empty. I didn't go into the encounter with much of anything on my mind a part from "what do I do now God?" His response was both surprising and sobering. "You asked me for the past year to get you away from that job and I delivered." In that moment God became the most real and personal He had been in our entire 14 year relationship.

During a time of prayer in the encounter we

were instructed to journal. The only thing God said was that it was time for my smile to be real. "You have been faking all your life. You've smiled and you've been hurting. Now it's time for you to smile from the inside; from my joy." God told me that I needed to come clean, particularly for Christians. This wasn't shocking, as my pastor's teaching had already made it evident that a lot of daily living and behavior issues were addressed to religious people in the bible and not to heathens; particularly through Apostle Paul's letters to the churches.

The demolition of the cover up had to start with me. I didn't understand that my freedom and restoration was an everyday process. I'd hidden behind my own wall of shame, too afraid to go up to anyone and admit that even in church I was battling depression. I'd been too ashamed to acknowledge openly that though I was saved and knew the word, I'd still been battling and walking things out. I'd been faithful in church, but still walking things out. I loved God, but even years later I was still struggling to redefine those negative things concerning myself that people had beat in me.

God spoke to me concerning the overwhelming number of people that are struggling in their Christian walks; hiding behind themselves and hiding behind the smile. They are hiding because they're still walking things out, and in many cases, still experiencing residual effects and backlash from past hurts and experiences. People aren't embracing the daily walk and daily commitment necessary for free living. Instead, they are hiding because they think anything less than appearing to have "arrived" is somehow ungodly or shameful. God said that just like me, people needed to know that affirming themselves and rebuilding their lives through the Word of God is a daily process.

From that life altering, wall shattering, captive freeing word, my company *Freedom Focused* was birthed and I was no longer afraid to tell my story.

Chapter 17...Let the Weak Say, "I Am Strong"

Wait on the LORD: be of good courage, and he shall strengthen thine heart: wait, I say, on the LORD.
                              Psalms 27:14 (KJV)

Mike Jenkins was named the 2011 United States World's Strongest Man, and although that sounds very impressive, the use of physical strength is not how you win in life. The Bible tells us that our battle is not against flesh and blood, but against principalities, against powers, against the rulers of the darkness of this world, against spiritual wickedness in high places (Eph. 6:12, KJV).

It takes great mental strength to wait on God with the hope that your situation is going to change. This type of patience is developed over time through prayer, teaching, counseling, and determination. A walk of faith is not for the weak or meek but for those who are convinced that there is more to life then what they are currently experiencing. I imagine my success and determination in this arena was in part due to the fact that I believed things had to get better for me and my family because they had already been so bad. I fought to hold on to the hope that all that I'd pushed passed, cried over, battled through and endured would eventually change for the better.

I had to believe the Word of God for myself, shut my mouth and ignore what my natural eyes could see. My eyes saw over due notices, disconnect alerts, empty cupboards and holes in the soles of my shoes. The same fight I carried concerning the well being of my children was the same fight I used to stand on the passages that flowed from the Bible. Each day got better; each week seemed calmer; each month held promise; and each year produced an outcome better then the year before. And although I couldn't say that I had "arrived", I had come to a place where I could recognize the hand of God moving in and through my life and the lives of my children. That was enough to keep me plowing through the messes of life and always maintaining expectations of the more and the greater...

Surprised? Did you expect a Hollywood ending and claims of total deliverance of a lifetime's worth of hurt in a few short years of being saved? Yes my life has improved tremendously, and apart from my relationship with God, I know none of it would have been possible. Still, what's important to me is that you understand that my life is only better because I embraced God's process. Sometimes healing doesn't come all at once, answered prayer doesn't come in an instant, and true happiness is achieved over time. The reality is that God restores broken lives that have been broken for generations. That type of healing doesn't happen overnight, but the beauty is that it happens.

Even after surrendering my life to Christ, I faced challenges. The difference is that I faced them with faith and a mountain moving God on my side instead of facing them alone. God took my surrendered life and all of its messes and broken pieces, those created by others and those self-inflicted, and He continues to perfect all things concerning me just as He promises in His word. He's been thorough and intentional in His healing of every hurt place, and over time, I stopped hiding behind my smile. God took my cover up, demolished it, and gave me a genuine peace and happiness that only comes from Him.

It's your turn now. What have you been hiding behind? True healing starts with transparency. Come out. There's strength for your weakness. There's beauty for your ashes. There's praise for your heaviness. There's healing for your hurt places. There's restoration for your broken pieces. There's true joy to replace your sorrow; and it's all found in Jesus Christ.

Chapter 18...Freedom Focused

In him and through faith in him we may approach
God with freedom and confidence.

Ephesians 3:12 (NIV)

Freedom is a journey, it's a lifestyle; not a destination. Perhaps the greatest enemy to freedom is assuming that you can "arrive" at this place called *There*, apart from heaven itself. This unrealistic expectation ends in disappointment the moment any of us makes a mistake or feels the pain of something we were so sure we'd left behind. Would I dare end such a tell-all story of my own life urging you not to make freedom your goal? Absolutely not. But I'd be leaving you ignorant concerning the reality of what freedom meant for me, and practical steps toward attaining it for yourselves if I don't make it very clear that you never arrive at freedom, you live it, each and every day.

There are no quick fixes or 12-step programs that are the cure all for years worth of hurt and disappointment, but these are practical steps for those who, like me, desire to live a continued lifestyle of freedom from past mistakes, abusers, and failures.

1. Forgiveness

Perhaps there is no greater hindering force than unforgiveness. There is nothing else that links you to the past quite like holding someone bondage in your heart for what they've done to you, or what you've done to yourself. We've all heard the saying, "harboring unforgiveness is like drinking poison and expecting someone else to die". This sobering truth is a clear picture of how toxic and deceptive bitterness and unforgiveness are. No one suffers apart from the one carrying it.

Some of you may argue, "you were molested, physically and verbally abused most of your life, abandoned by your father, neglected by your mother, hurt by the church"; if anyone had a right to be angry with at least a few key people for the rest of their life it should have been me, right? I had to realize that no matter what happened in my past, if I was willing to release the past and everyone in it, the best days of my life were still ahead of me. So I became a liberal forgiver, even writing letters when necessary.

Once I made the decision to forgive those that had hurt me, I moved on to a harder task; forgiving myself. It often seems as though we muster the strength to forgive others far more easily than we are willing to forgive ourselves.

Still, unforgiveness toward yourself is just as toxic as bitterness and unforgiveness toward others. So without basing forgiveness on feelings or emotions, because forgiveness is simply a choice, I made a decision. I released myself from every bad decision, every wrong turn, and every failure. I decided to embrace the fresh start God had for me, and so did my children. Each time the pasts tries to knock on my door, I remind it that I left it behind years ago.

2. Sharing With Someone You Trust

Nothing keeps you in bondage quite like a secret, and nothing is more liberating and therapeutic than coming clean. Hiding your past like it will one day vanish is not only irrational, but it would mean everything God has allowed you to see the other side of is in vain. Where is the freedom and liberty in hiding? Who benefits from a testimony left untold? The bible makes it clear that we overcome not by burying our pasts, but by the blood of the lamb and the words of our testimony.

I encourage you to find a friend you can trust and share your story. I can attest to the new level of freedom and healing from my past that's come each time I've been unashamed to share. I eventually arrived at a place of wholeness that allowed me to write this book, believing that my transparency can now be used by God to set multitudes of people free. There's no greater satisfaction than knowing that in spite of everything I've gone through, nothing has been in vain, and I assure you, your testimony is not in vain either. Every hurt, every failure, every tear you've shed, God has record of each of them, and He's promised to work every one into His plan for your good.

3. Acknowledging Imperfections

Perhaps the biggest favor you can do yourself along this journey to freedom is acknowledging your imperfections and settling that perfection is unattainable. YOU WILL MAKE MISTAKES, and that's okay. God is not surprised, and you shouldn't be either. As believers, we spend so much time beating ourselves up for everything we're not that we don't maximize everything we are. The bible says that God's grace is sufficient for you, and that His strength is made perfect in weakness. Embrace your weaknesses as opportunities for God's strength to be put on display through your life in ways only He can take credit for.

If everyone God chose was perfect, how mighty of a God would it take to save them? If everyone God used was strong, how powerful would God have to be to ensure their victory? No, God chooses the weak, the meek, the broken, the sinful; and He shows himself all-powerful through their ordinary lives. It's God that makes us extraordinary. Accept that if you were perfect you'd cease to need a savior, and I can't speak for you, but I don't want my home in heaven dependent upon my ability to achieve perfection in this life.

4. Seeking Help (Therapy, Books, Etc.)

Don't ever be ashamed to ask for or pursue help. Never underestimate the resources God will use to heal, deliver, and set you free. We often cry out to God for help, expecting something from the sci-fi network to appear in our living rooms. Nothing is impossible for God, but I assure you, many can attest to how practical God's help is.

You may find that a book such as this one helps you along your freedom journey. You may find that talking to a counselor or therapist helps uncover suppressed memories and emotions hindering your total deliverance. In many cases, especially those of us whose pain or abuse dates back to childhood, we find that we alone were not responsible for creating the problems in our lives; that said, don't be so quick to assume that you have to walk out of them alone either. Ask for help, pick up resources, and know that whatever works along your journey is a blessing.

5. Extending Grace to Yourself

Learn to celebrate even the smallest of accomplishments in your life, and know that although you'll continue to be imperfect and make mistakes, you are still very much loved by God. Continue being a liberal forgiver with yourself, and don't get caught up in the opinions of others. Ultimately, God's opinion of you is what matters, and He's already promised you are forgiven and loved. Continuing the journey of freedom without regard for the opinions of people allows God to use us for His work, and it inspires a boldness that makes our lives fulfilling.

Maybe you're reading this and don't necessarily share in my testimony. I'm grateful for that. Still, this is no less your call to action. My desire is that sensitivity and compassion would be awakened in each of us. My story is simply one of many. It's time we possess a heightened sensitivity to the issues of those we encounter each day, both inside and outside of the church. May we embrace a compassion that moves us to see what's behind the smile, and to hear what people don't say. It's only through such sensitivity and compassion that we'll effectively be used as the hands that deliver the healing touches of God to a hurting and broken world.

www.ingramcontent.com/pod-product-compliance
Lightning Source LLC
Chambersburg PA
CBHW060137050426
42448CB00010B/2180